TIME FOR
OUTRAGE

TIME FOR OUTRAGE

Indignez-vous!

STÉPHANE HESSEL

Translated by Marion Duvert

TWELVE

NEW YORK BOSTON

Twelve
Hachette Book Group
237 Park Avenue
New York, NY 10017

www.HachetteBookGroup.com

Twelve is an imprint of Grand Central Publishing.
The Twelve name and logo are trademarks of
Hachette Book Group, Inc.

The publisher is not responsible for websites (or their
content) that are not owned by the publisher.

Printed in the United States of America

First North American Edition: September 2011
10 9 8 7 6 5 4 3 2 1

ISBN: 978-1-4555-0972-0

TIME FOR
OUTRAGE

Time for Outrage

Ninety-three years old. The last leg of my journey. The end is in sight. I'm lucky to be able to seize the time I have left to reflect on the events that laid the foundation for my lifelong commitment to politics: the Resistance, and the program devised sixty-six years ago by the National Council of the Resistance. For this, we owe a debt of gratitude to Jean Moulin, who rallied together the scattered forces that opposed the German occupation of France—resistance movements, political parties, trade unions—to unite them in their defense of France and their pledge of allegiance to its only true leader: General Charles de Gaulle. I had joined de Gaulle in London in March 1941. And it was there, on

March 15, 1944, that I learned the council had drawn up and adopted a declaration of its policy, putting forward a set of values and principles upon which to ground our nation's modern democracy once it was freed from occupation.[1]

Today, more than ever, we need these principles and values. It is the duty of us all to ensure that our society remain one of which we are proud, not a society wary of immigrants and intent on their expulsion or a society that disputes the welfare state or a society in which the media are controlled by the wealthy. We would oppose such things were we the true heirs to the National Council of the Resistance.

The year 1945 marked the end of a horrific tragedy. It also marked the beginning of an ambitious plan for the renewal of society, driven by the forces that made up the council. Let us not forget that this was when French Social Security came into being, just as the Resistance had stipulated in its program: "a far-reaching Social Security system, guaranteeing that no citizen would go without the basic means to survive should he or she be unable to work";

"a pension allowing workers to end their days in dignity."

Energy—electricity, gas, and coal—was nationalized. So were the major banks, for this was what the program advocated: "that the nation reclaim all major means of production thus far monopolized, the fruit of the workers' labor; all sources of energy; the riches of our natural resources; the insurance companies and the largest banks"; "that a true democracy, both economic and social, be established, which implies the eradication of the economic and financial feudalism ruling our economy." Common interest would prevail over individual interest, just as the fair sharing of proceeds between workers would override the power of money. The Resistance proposed "a rational reorganization of the economy that would ensure the subordination of individual interest to the common interest, a structure freed from the dictatorship of executives that is but a replica of the fascist state," and the Provisional Government of the French Republic (1944–46) acted as a channel for these proposals.

A true democracy requires and insists on freedom of the press; the Resistance understood this, and it made its demands accordingly. It supported "the freedom of the press, its honor and its independence from the state, from the power of capital and from foreign influence." As early as 1944, the government passed legislation to ensure these freedoms. Today, however, these freedoms are once again in peril.

The Resistance called for "all French children to receive a thorough education" without discrimination. Yet reforms proposed in France in 2008 endanger this plan. A number of young teachers, whose actions I champion, have gone so far as to refuse to apply them. Their salaries were cut as punishment. Their sense of outrage flared up; they "disobeyed," judging these reforms to be disloyal to the ideals of the republic, serving instead a money-driven society that hinders the development of creativity and the spirit of debate.

Today, it is the very foundation of the social achievements of the Resistance that is under fire.[2]

Indignation
Fuels Resistance

We are told, shamelessly, that the state cannot bear the costs of certain civil measures any longer. But how can we lack the funds to maintain these programs when our nations enjoy greater wealth than at any time since the Liberation, when Europe lay in ruins? How else to explain this but by the corrupting power of money, which the Resistance fought so fiercely against, and which is now greater, more insolent, and more selfish than ever.

The wealthy have installed their slaves in the highest spheres of the state. The banks are privately owned. They are concerned solely with profits. They have no interest in the common good. The gap between rich and poor is the widest it's ever been; the pursuit of riches and the spirit of competition are encouraged and celebrated.

The basic motive of the Resistance was indignation. We, veterans of the French Resistance and the combat forces that freed our country, call on you, our younger generations, to revive and carry forward the heritage and ideals of the Resistance. Here is our message: It's time to take over! It's time to get angry! Politicians, economists, intellectuals, do not surrender! The true fabric of our society remains strong. Let us not be defeated by the tyranny of the world financial markets that threaten peace and democracy everywhere.

I wish all of you to find your reason for indignation. This is a precious thing. When outraged, as I was by Nazism, you will become militant, strong, and engaged. You will join the great course of history as it flows toward greater justice, greater freedom—but not the reckless freedom of the fox in the henhouse. In 1948, the General Assembly of the United Nations proclaimed a Universal Declaration of Human Rights. If you encounter someone who is robbed of these rights, pity her, and help her claim those rights.

Two Visions
of History

When I try to understand the origins of
fascism—what caused France to fall
under the domination of the Vichy regime—I
tell myself that the wealthy, in their selfishness,
were terrified of the Bolsheviks. They were
driven by fear. What we need today, just as we
needed then, is for a segment of the population
to rise up in protest. A minority is all we need,
like yeast to the dough.

Of course, I am an old man now, and my
experience is so different from that of today's
youth. When I visit high schools, I tell students
that their reasons for political engagement aren't
as obvious as mine were. For us, resisting meant
refusing German occupation, repudiating defeat.

It was relatively simple, as was what followed: decolonization, and the Algerian War. Algeria had to become independent, it was clear. As for Stalin, we all cheered when the Red Army defeated the Nazis in 1943. But as early as 1935, when we were first hearing about the trials and the Great Purge—and even as we had to lend a favorable ear to communism in order to counterbalance American capitalism—the need to oppose totalitarianism was self-evident.

My long life has provided me with many reasons to feel outraged. But my indignation was born less of emotion than of a deep desire to *engage*. Jean-Paul Sartre made a very strong impression on me when I was a student at the École Normale Supérieure. *Nausea* and *The Wall* were crucial in the formation of my ideology. Sartre taught us the following: "As individuals, you are responsible." It was a libertarian message. The responsibility is that of the individual who will rely neither on a form of power nor on a god. You must engage—your humanity demands it. When, in 1939, I started at the École Normale on rue d'Ulm in Paris,

I was a fervent disciple of the philosopher Hegel, and I also attended Maurice Merleau-Ponty's seminars. His lectures examined concrete experience, that of the body in relationship to sense (*sense* in the singular form; i.e., *meaning* as opposed to the physical senses). As an optimist, I felt that what was desirable should be possible, so I found Hegel compelling. In Hegel's interpretation, the history of humanity has a pattern. History is formed by a series of shocks—great disruptions to society that humanity must confront and correct in order to achieve an increase in freedoms. Only when man accedes to complete freedom can we have a democratic state in its ideal form.

Of course, one can view history differently. Progress—the advance of freedom, competition, the constant quest for more and better—can be perceived as a storm of destruction. This is how history was depicted by a friend of my father's, the man with whom he shared the task of translating Marcel Proust's *In Search of Lost Time* into German: the German philosopher Walter Benjamin. Benjamin had a pessimistic interpretation of a work by the Swiss painter Paul Klee, *Angelus Novus*, in which an angel spreads its arms as if to contain and fight off a tempest that Benjamin identified as Progress. For the philosopher, who would commit suicide in September 1940 to escape the Nazis, the design of history was not a progression but a relentless, devastating march from one catastrophe to another.

The Worst Attitude
Is Indifference

It is true, the reasons to get angry may seem less clear today, and the world may seem more complex. Who is in charge; who are the decision makers? It's not always easy to discern. We're not dealing with a small elite anymore, whose actions we can clearly identify. We are dealing with a vast, interdependent world that is interconnected in unprecedented ways. But there are unbearable things all around us. You have to look for them; search carefully. Open your eyes and you will see. This is what I tell young people: If you spend a little time searching, you will find your reasons to engage. The worst attitude is indifference. "There's nothing I can do; I get by"—adopting this mindset will deprive you of one of the fundamental qualities of being human: outrage. Our capacity for protest is indispensable, as is our freedom to engage.

We can already identify two major challenges:

1. The grievous injustices inflicted on people deprived of the essential requirements for a decent life, not only in the third world—in Africa, Asia, Haiti, and elsewhere—but in the suburbs of our largest Western cities, where seclusion and poverty breeds hatred and revolt. The widening gap between the very poor and very rich is made all the more insulting by the access the poor now have to the internet and other forms of mass communication that highlight these inequalities.

2. The violation of basic freedoms and fundamental rights. In his 1941 State of the Union speech, Franklin Delano Roosevelt articulated the "Four Freedoms" he felt people "everywhere in the world" had a right to enjoy: Freedom of Speech, Freedom of Worship,

Freedom from Want, and Freedom from Fear. It was in support of these very principles that Roosevelt decided to enter the Second World War. The Four Freedoms later served as the foundation for the charter of the United Nations, which was adopted in San Francisco on June 24, 1945, and served as the inspiration for the UN's Universal Declaration of Human Rights, drafted under the chairmanship of FDR's widow, Eleanor Roosevelt. It was my privilege to be associated with the drafting of the declaration, which was adopted by the United Nations on December 10, 1948, at the Palais de Chaillot in Paris. I was chief of staff for Henri Laugier, then assistant secretary-general of the United Nations and secretary of the United Nations Commission on Human Rights, and as such I participated, with others, in writing the declaration. I will never forget the crucial role played by Eleanor Roosevelt, whose great kindness and natural authority worked wonders to help reconcile the disparate personalities that comprised the commission. She was a vibrant feminist, and it is largely due to her that, for the very first time, and on a global scale, the equality of men and women was inscribed without ambiguity in an official text. Article II of the declaration is absolutely explicit on this matter. René Cassin, who had been in charge of the departments of Justice and Education for the Free French government-in-exile in London in 1941, and who would be awarded the Nobel Peace Prize in 1968, played an equally important role, as did Pierre Mendès-France, then a member of the Economic and Social Council, to whom our drafts were submitted for approval before they were further examined by the Third Committee, which focused on social, humanitarian affairs and human-rights issues. The committee included what were at the time all fifty-four member countries of the United Nations, and I was its acting secretary. We owe the term *universal rights* to René Cassin, who insisted on it rather than *international*, as was first proposed by our Anglophone friends. The stakes were high in the immediate aftermath of World War II: humanity had to eradicate the menace of totalitarianism. This could be achieved only if the member countries of the United Nations committed themselves to respecting *universal* rights. This was a way of disarming the argument of sovereignty that a state might appeal to while perpetrating crimes against humanity on its own soil—as Hitler did. He believed his supreme authority at home gave him license to commit genocide. The Universal Declaration owes much to the revulsion universally felt toward Nazism, fascism, and totalitarianism—and it owes much, through our presence, to the spirit of the Resistance. I had the sense that we needed to act fast, that we should not be fooled by the hypocrisies of the victors, not all of whom were intent on loyally promoting the values to which they were swearing allegiance and that we were trying to impose.[3]

I can't resist quoting from Article 15 of the Universal Declaration of Human Rights: "Everyone has the right to a nationality." And from Article 22: "Everyone, as a member of society, has the right to social security and is entitled to realization, through national effort and international cooperation and in accordance with the organization and resources of each state, of the economic, social, and cultural rights indispensable for his dignity and the free development of his personality." And while the declaration itself is not legally binding, it has nevertheless played a powerful role since 1948: we have seen colonized people appeal to it as they demanded independence; it has been the seed in the minds of the oppressed as they fought for freedom.

It's been cheering to see more and more nongovernmental organizations and social movements appear in the past few decades—groups such as the Association for the Taxation of Financial Transactions and for Citizens' Action (also known as ATTAC in its French acronym), the International Federation for Human Rights, Amnesty International, and others—all of them dynamic, efficient groups. To achieve their goals, these organizations have had to function as a network, making the most of today's extensive means of communication.

To the youth, I say again: look around you and you will find the themes to justify your indignation—the treatment of immigrants, the expulsion of illegal workers, the dismantling of Roma camps in some European countries.* You will become aware of situations so deplorable they simply demand civil action. Seek and you will find!

---

* The Roma, also known as Gypsies, are an ethnic group that migrated from northern India centuries ago and has since become widely dispersed in Europe and elsewhere.

Palestine

My Own Outrage

Today I am most outraged by the situation in Palestine, Gaza, and the West Bank. The source of my indignation is inspired by the call from courageous Israelis to us Jews living abroad: you, our brothers, come and see where our leaders have taken our country, oblivious of the fundamental humane values of Judaism. I went to Gaza in 2002 and returned five times over the next seven years.

The September 2009 Goldstone Report, by South African judge Richard Goldstone, himself a Jew and even a Zionist, is an essential read. It was commissioned by the United Nations to investigate the situation in the Gaza Strip. In the report, Goldstone accuses the Israeli army of having committed "acts [that] would constitute war crimes and may amount to crimes against humanity" during its three-week Operation Cast Lead. Goldstone's recent expression of regret for having overstated his condemnation cannot be taken seriously. In 2009, in order to see with our own eyes what the report described, my wife and I went back to Gaza, where we were free to travel thanks to our diplomatic passports. The people traveling with us, though, were not permitted to enter the Gaza Strip or the West Bank. We visited some refugee camps established as early as 1948 by the UNRWA (United Nations Relief and Works Agency for Palestine Refugees in the Near East), where more than three million Palestinians are waiting to reclaim the land Israel forced them to abandon, while their possible return becomes more and more problematic. As for Gaza itself, it is an open-air prison for one and a half million Palestinians. We saw the physical destruction caused by Cast Lead—the wreckage of the al-Quds Hospital being a case in point—but what we will forever remember is the inhabitants of Gaza themselves. Their attitude, their patriotism, their love of the sea and the beach, their constant attention to their children's well-being—such delightful swarms of laughing children. We were impressed by the ingenious ways they coped with the scarcity imposed on them. We saw them make bricks, for lack of cement, to rebuild the thousands of houses demolished by Israeli tanks. We received confirmation that fourteen hundred Palestinians died during Operation Cast Lead—women, children, and the elderly among them—while only fifty people were injured on the Israeli side. That Jews themselves might be perpetrating war crimes is unbearable to me. Alas, there are few examples in history, if any, of populations who draw lessons from their own past.

President Obama, whose Cairo speech had raised so many hopes, has been a great disappointment in his response to this problem. I am well aware that Hamas, winner of the last election, was unable to prevent rocket attacks on Israeli cities. They were conducted in response to Gaza's isolation, and to the Israeli blockade of the strip. Of course, I consider terrorism intolerable. But when a population is occupied by a much superior military force, its reaction cannot be strictly nonviolent.

Does Hamas benefit from rocket attacks on the city of Sderot? No. Such gestures do not serve Hamas's cause, but one can argue that they're the consequences of Gaza's exasperation. Violence inspired by exasperation is too often the outcome of unacceptable situations. In this light, one can see terrorism itself as a form of exasperation—and, as such, "exasperation" becomes a negative term. Instead of exasperation, there should be aspiration. Exasperation negates hope. As an emotion, it is understandable. I might even go so far as to say that it is natural. But it is nonetheless unacceptable, because it will never accomplish what hope could.

Do not misunderstand me: I stand in solidarity with Jews in Israel and around the world, because I know what it is to be a Jew. I am myself of Jewish origin, and I unequivocally

support the idea that Jews, after all they've
suffered, deserve a country of their own. I
shouted with joy when Israel was founded.
I said, "At last!" And to my critics, I repeat:
my love for Israel is stronger than yours. But I
want it to be an honest country. Some people
react emotionally to my criticism of Israel, but
I don't understand why. I am a believer in the
universality of human rights. And I believe
that when the government of Israel occupies
Palestinian territories, it does so in violation
of the principles put forward by the United
Nations in 1967. It is breaking laws. And it
must be criticized for it, as any other state
doing so should be criticized. Israel is not above
international laws.

Nonviolence

The Path We Must Learn to Follow

I am convinced that the future belongs to nonviolence and the reconciliation of clashing cultures. This is how humanity will take its next step forward. And this is where Sartre and I meet: there is no *excusing* terrorists who throw bombs, but we can *understand* them. Sartre wrote, in 1947: "I recognize that violence, in whichever form it manifests itself, is a failure. But it is an unavoidable failure, because we live in a world of violence. And while it is true that the risk of resorting to violence against violence is that it may only perpetuate violence, it is also true that it is the only way to put an end to it."[4] To which I would say that nonviolence is a more reliable method to end violence.

One cannot lend one's support to terrorists, as Sartre did during the Algerian War or the 1972 Summer Olympics, when eleven Israeli athletes lost their lives in the Munich massacre. This is untenable; Sartre himself would come to question the value and meaning of terrorism toward the end of his life. To tell oneself that violence is ineffective is much more important than to wonder whether to condemn those who commit it. Terrorism doesn't work. If there is such a thing as violent hope, then it is to be found in Guillaume Apollinaire's poetry—"How slow life is; How violent hope is"—not in politics. In March 1980, three weeks before his death, Sartre conceded: "We must try to explain that our contemporary world, in all its horror, is just one moment in the long development of history; that hope has always been one of the dominant forces in revolutions and insurrections; and that I continue to hold hope as my conception of the future."[5]

It must be understood that violence turns its back on hope. Hopefulness and the hope for nonviolence must be favored over violence. This is the path we must learn to follow. Oppressors and the oppressed alike must reach out to each other to eradicate oppression; only this will put an end to terrorist violence. We must not let hatred build up and take over.

The messages of Gandhi, Martin Luther King Jr., and Nelson Mandela remain relevant even in a world where ideological confrontations and invasive totalitarianism have been overcome. They are messages of hope, of faith in a society's ability to overcome conflict through mutual understanding and watchful patience. To achieve this, we must rely on our belief in human rights, the violation of which—whoever the perpetrators may be—must provoke our indignation. We must never surrender these rights.

For a Peaceful Insurrection

I'm not the only one to have bristled at the Israeli government's response to the peaceful demonstrations organized by the citizens of Bil'in, a small village in the West Bank. Each Friday, they walk down to the site of the wall and there, without throwing stones, without using force, they protest against Israel's annexation of their land. The Israeli authorities have classified this march as "nonviolent terrorism." Not bad. You would have to be Israeli to label nonviolence as terrorism. More important, you'd have to be embarrassed by the effectiveness of nonviolence, which elicits support, understanding, and encouragement from all those around the world who are against oppression.

The Western obsession with productivity and the accumulation of wealth has led the world into a crisis. To come out of it, we need a radical departure from this constant rush forward—the constant quest for more and better—that we've been carrying out not only in the financial world, but also in the realms of science and technology. It is high time that integrity, justice, and sustainable development be allowed to prevail. There are grave issues. Our adventure on Earth is imperiled, and should man persist in making the planet uninhabitable it will come to an end.

Nevertheless, substantial progress has been made since 1948: we've seen decolonization, the end of Apartheid, the destruction of the Soviet empire, the fall of the Berlin Wall. But in the first ten years of the twenty-first century, we've been backsliding. I believe this is explained in part by the Bush presidency and the disastrous ways the United States responded to the September 11 attacks, such as the deployment of troops to Iraq. We've endured an economic crisis, and still we have no policies that would prevent it from happening again. Similarly, the Copenhagen summit on climate change has failed to bring about concrete measures to preserve the environment. We are on a threshold between the horrors of the first decade of this century and the prospects of the decades to come.

But let's be hopeful—we must never lose hope. The 1990s saw some tremendous developments, with the United Nations convening conferences like the first international Earth Summit in Rio in 1992 and the Beijing World Conference on Women in 1995. In September 2000 the 191 member countries adopted the eight Millennium Development Goals initiated by UN secretary-general Kofi Annan, committing their nations to reducing world poverty by half by the year 2015. To my great regret, neither Obama nor the European Union has come forward yet with proposals for what their contribution should be to a new, constructive phase in which our fundamental values are further enshrined. But hope is rising again: the Arab Spring promises democratic change that all of us throughout the world should passionately encourage.

How can I conclude this call for indignation?

By reiterating that on the sixtieth anniversary of the Program of the National Council of the Resistance—March 8, 2004—we, veterans of the Resistance who fought for Free France between 1940 and 1945, said the following: "Yes, Nazism was defeated, thanks to our brothers and sisters of the Resistance who sacrificed their lives, and thanks to the nations united in their opposition to fascist barbarity. But the threat persists; we are not entirely rid of it. And against injustice, our anger remains intact."[6]

Indeed, the threat persists. We therefore maintain our call for "a rebellion—peaceful and resolute—against the instruments of mass media that offer our young people a worldview defined by the temptations of mass consumption, a disdain for the weak, and a contempt for culture, historical amnesia, and the relentless competition of all against all."

To the men and women who will make the twenty-first century, we say with affection:

> "TO CREATE IS TO RESIST.
> TO RESIST IS TO CREATE."

Publisher's Notes

1. The National Council of the Resistance (CNR) was founded clandestinely on May 27, 1943, in Paris by the representatives of the eight major movements that made up the Resistance. This included members of the two largest prewar trade unions, the CGT (General Confederation of Labor) and the CFTC (French Confederation of Christian Workers); and by the six major parties of the Third Republic, including the PC (Communist Party) and the SFIO (the Socialists). The CNR held its first meeting on that very day under the presidency of Jean Moulin, who had been appointed by General de Gaulle. It was de Gaulle's hope that the CNR would fight Nazism more efficiently, thereby reinforcing his own legitimacy in the eyes of the Allied forces. He asked the CNR to devise a government program in anticipation of the liberation

of France. After some back-and-forth between the CNR and the government for Free France—which was based both in London and Algiers—the program was adopted on March 15, 1944, and handed to General de Gaulle in a ceremony held at the City Hall in Paris on August 25, 1944. It's worth noting that the legislation having to do with freedom of the press was passed as early as August 26, and that Roger Ginsburger, the son of a rabbi from Alsace, held one of the most significant roles in drafting the program. Under the pseudonym Pierre Villon, he acted as secretary-general of the National Front for the Independence of France—a movement created by the French Communist Party in 1941—and represented this movement within the CNR and its permanent bureau.

2. According to a trade union estimate, retirement plans have lowered their coverage of net wages from a level of 75 percent or 80 percent to roughly 50 percent. In 2010, Jean-Paul Domin, a professor of economics at Université de Reims Champagne-Ardennes, wrote a report for the European Institute on the Salariat about Assurance Maladie Complémentaire. Privately funded, Assurance Maladie Complémentaire is an employer-provided insurance plan that complements universal health care, from which everyone in France—whether fully employed or not—benefits. In

his report, Jean-Paul Domin demonstrates the ways in which the quality of coverage for Assurance Maladie Complémentaire is now directly tied to a recipient's level of employment and compensation; in other words, those in precarious professional situations have had to forgo some medical treatments for lack of Assurance Maladie Complémentaire. Money has taken precedence over the very social rights that were central to the legislation passed on October 4 and October 15, 1945. This legislation promoted Social Security and determined that it would be regulated by two entities: the state, and the workers (through their representatives). With the Juppé reforms in 1995 and the Douste-Blazy law of 2004, Social Security has fallen under the management of the state only. The president of Caisse Nationale d'Assurance Maladie (CNAM), for instance, is now appointed by the French president. After the Liberation, trade unions headed the departmental branches of the CNAM, which is no longer the case: now, the unions merely act in an advisory capacity.

3. The Universal Declaration of Human Rights was adopted by the General Assembly of the United Nations on December 10, 1948, at the Palais de Chaillot in Paris. Forty-eight out of the fifty-eight member nations ratified the text. Eight abstained: South Africa,

because of Apartheid (which the declaration condemned de facto); Saudi Arabia, similarly, because of gender inequality; the USSR (Russia, Ukraine, Belorussia), Poland, Czechoslovakia, and Yugoslavia, which believed that the declaration wasn't adamant enough on the economic and social fronts, or on questions of minority rights. It is worth noting that Russia was particularly assertive in opposing an Australian proposal to found an international court of human rights that would examine the petitions brought to the UN's attention. Article 8 of the declaration—"Everyone has the right to an effective remedy by the competent national tribunals for acts violating the fundamental rights granted him by the constitution or by law"—allows an individual to sue a state. This principle would come into play in Europe in 1998 with the creation of the European Court of Human Rights, which secures this right for more than five hundred million Europeans.

4. Jean-Paul Sartre, "Situation of the Writer in 1947," in *Situations II* (Paris: Gallimard, 1948).

5. Jean-Paul Sartre, "Maintenant l'espoir…(III)," in *Le Nouvel Observateur*, March 24, 1980.

6. The signatories of the Appeal of March 8, 2004, were: Lucie Aubrac, Raymond Aubrac, Henry Bartoli, Daniel Cordier, Philippe Dechartre, Georges Guingouin, Stéphane Hessel, Maurice Kriegel-Valrimont,

Lise London, Georges Séguy, Germaine Tillion, Jean-Pierre Vernant, Maurice Voutey. This appeal resonated very strongly among the younger generations, as did Stéphane Hessel's improvised speech on May 17, 2009, at the annual meeting "Paroles de Résistance" (Resisting in Words and Actions) presented by the nonprofit organization "Citoyens Résistants d'Hier et d'Aujourd'hui" (Citizen Resistance Fighters of Yesterday and Today). Reminding the crowd that indignation had been the motive of the Resistance, Hessel said: "Find your own reasons to get angry, and join the great flow of history!" This intervention, recorded by filmmaker Gilles Perret for his movie *Walter, or the Return to Resistance*, served as the starting point for the book published here. More information about this organization can be found at www.citoyens-resistants.fr.

About the Author

Stéphane Hessel was born in Berlin in 1917 to Franz Hessel, a German-Jewish writer and translator; and Helen Grund, a painter, musician, and writer. The couple moved to Paris in 1924 with their two children, Ulrich (the elder) and Stéphane. Growing up in an artistic household, the boys came to know the Parisian avant-garde—the Dadaist painter Marcel Duchamp and the sculptor Alexander Calder, notably, were friends of the family. Stéphane was admitted to the École Normale Supérieure on rue d'Ulm in Paris in 1939, but his studies were interrupted by the war. Naturalized as a French citizen since 1937, he was drafted into the French Army and fought in the Phoney War.

He left France upon learning that Maréchal Philippe Pétain was yielding the country's sovereignty, and subsequently joined General de Gaulle's Free French Forces in London in March 1941.

In this period, Hessel worked at the Central Bureau of Intelligence and Operations, commonly referred to as the BCRA. In late March 1944, he was dispatched to France, where he landed clandestinely and commenced operations under the code name Greco. His mission was to establish communication with the various Resistance movements in Paris, and to find new locations from which to broadcast information to London in preparation for the Allied invasion. On July 10, 1944, he was betrayed to the Gestapo and captured in Paris. He wrote in his memoirs *Dance with the Century*, published in 1997, that there should be "no prosecution against those who speak under torture." Hessel himself was interrogated and tortured—by waterboarding, in particular—but his command of the German language disconcerted his torturers. On August 8, 1944, mere days before the Liberation of Paris, he was sent to the Buchenwald concentration camp in Germany, where he was sentenced to death by hanging. On the eve of his execution, he managed to exchange his identity with that of a Frenchman who had died of typhus in the camp. And under his new name, Michel Boitel—a miller by profession—he was transferred to the Rottleberode camp, near the factory where Germany produced the undercarriage for the Junkers Ju 52 airplane. Luckily (in another testament to Hessel's unfaltering good fortune) he was placed in the accounting department.

He tried unsuccessfully to escape and was transferred to the Dora camp, where the V-1 and V-2 flying bombs—the missiles with which the Nazis still hoped to win the war— were manufactured. He was assigned to the disciplinary company and escaped again, this time successfully, as the troops of the Allied forces were approaching Dora. And at long last he returned to Paris, where he reunited with his wife, Vitia, the mother of his two sons and daughter.

"I had reclaimed my life, and was intent on living an engaged existence," he wrote in his memoirs, describing this period.

In 1946, he was admitted to the Ministry of Foreign Affairs and became a diplomat. His first appointment was at the United Nations, where Henri Laugier, assistant secretary-general of the United Nations and secretary of the United Nations Commission on Human Rights, asked Hessel to serve as his chief of staff. It was in this position that Hessel joined the committee in charge of drafting what became the Universal Declaration of Human Rights. Among the twelve members of the committee, six played a crucial role. Eleanor Roosevelt, widow of President Roosevelt, a feminist and a lifelong human-rights advocate, chaired the committee. Dr. Peng Chung Chang (from Kuomintang China), vice chairman of the committee, said that the declaration should reflect not only Western but also Eastern ideas. Charles Habib Malik (Lebanon), committee rapporteur, is often characterized, along with Eleanor Roosevelt, as the driving force for the

declaration's adoption. René Cassin (France),
a jurist and a diplomat, was president of the
French National Consultative Commission on
Human Rights. He drafted several articles of
the declaration, and his response to the fear
expressed by some states (France included)
that the declaration might imperil their
colonial sovereignty was remarkable. Cassin
was ambitious, undeterred, and in favor of
interventionism. John Peters Humphrey
(Canada), a lawyer and a diplomat, was a close
collaborator of Laugier's. He wrote the first
four-hundred-page draft of the declaration. And
finally, there was Stéphane Hessel, diplomat and
Laugier's chief of staff, the youngest of all the
members. The spirit of the Resistance clearly
ruled over the committee.

The declaration was adopted by the
United Nations on December 10, 1948, at
the Palais de Chaillot in Paris. In the years
that followed, the United Nations saw a flood
of new officers seeking lucrative positions.
This shift marginalized those who, as Hessel
recalls in his memoirs, "strived to impose their

ideals." Hessel left the United Nations and was appointed by the Ministry of Foreign Affairs as a representative of France in a number of international institutions—thus giving him the chance to return to New York and the United Nations for a brief period of time. He actively supported Algeria's independence during the Algerian War. And in 1977, thanks in part to Secretary-General of the Elysée Claude Brossolette (the son of Pierre Brossolette, who had been the director of the BCRA) Hessel was offered the position of French ambassador at the United Nations in Geneva by President Valéry Giscard d'Estaing.

Hessel was characteristically upfront about this: of all the French politicians, it was with Pierre Mendès-France that Hessel felt the greatest affinity. They had met in London at the time of the Free French Forces, and again in New York in 1946 at the United Nations, where Mendès-France represented their country in the Economic and Social Council. As he would later write, Hessel owed the consecration of his career as a diplomat to the "deep metamorphosis

France underwent when François Mitterrand became president" in 1981. "Under Mitterrand, I went from being a functional diplomat, rather narrowly specialized in multilateral cooperation, to a French ambassador." Hessel later joined the Socialist Party.

"Why? I wonder. My immediate answer is: the shock of 1995. I would have never thought the French population could be so reckless as to elect Jacques Chirac president." Hessel and his new wife, who at this time held diplomatic passports, visited the Gaza Strip in 2008 and 2009. He attested to the painful struggle of Gaza's inhabitants. And around that time, he declared the following: "I have always sided with the dissidents."

This is, indeed, the very same man who speaks here at age ninety-three.

SC